T0197425

Boys Will Be Boys
Girls Will Be Girls

Ellie Owen

Complimentary teaching resources for this book are available at EllieOwenBooks.wordpress.com.

This book belongs to

WestBow Press books may be ordered through booksellers or by contacting:

WestBow Press
A Division of Thomas Nelson & Zondervan
1663 Liberty Drive
Bloomington, IN 47403
www.westbowpress.com
844-714-3454

Because of the dynamic nature of the Internet, any web addresses or links contained in this
book may have changed since publication and may no longer be valid. The views expressed
in this work are solely those of the author and do not necessarily reflect the views of
the publisher, and the publisher hereby disclaims any responsibility for them.

ISBN: 978-1-6642-5669-9 (sc)
ISBN: 978-1-6642-5671-2 (hc)
ISBN: 978-1-6642-5670-5 (e)

Library of Congress Control Number: 2022901845

Print information available on the last page.

WestBow Press rev. date: 2/21/2022

WESTBOW
P R E S S®
A DIVISION OF THOMAS NELSON
& ZONDERVAN

Boys Will Be Boys

Ellie Owen

I've been a boy
since God first thought me up,
even before I was born.
Since the God of the Universe
planned this for me,
it's not something
I want to scorn.

My boyhood is central
to the person I am
in my body, my heart
and my mind,
It's a basic component
God put into me
when my character He designed.

You see, back at the start
when God made the first people,
His own likeness He let them display.
And the man and the woman
together did this,
and it's still that way today.

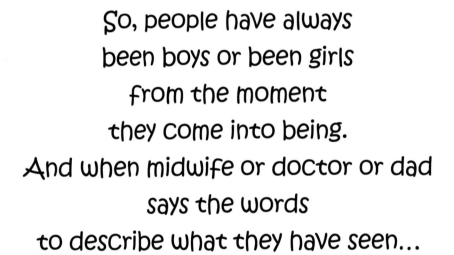

So, people have always
been boys or been girls
from the moment
they come into being.
And when midwife or doctor or dad
says the words
to describe what they have seen...

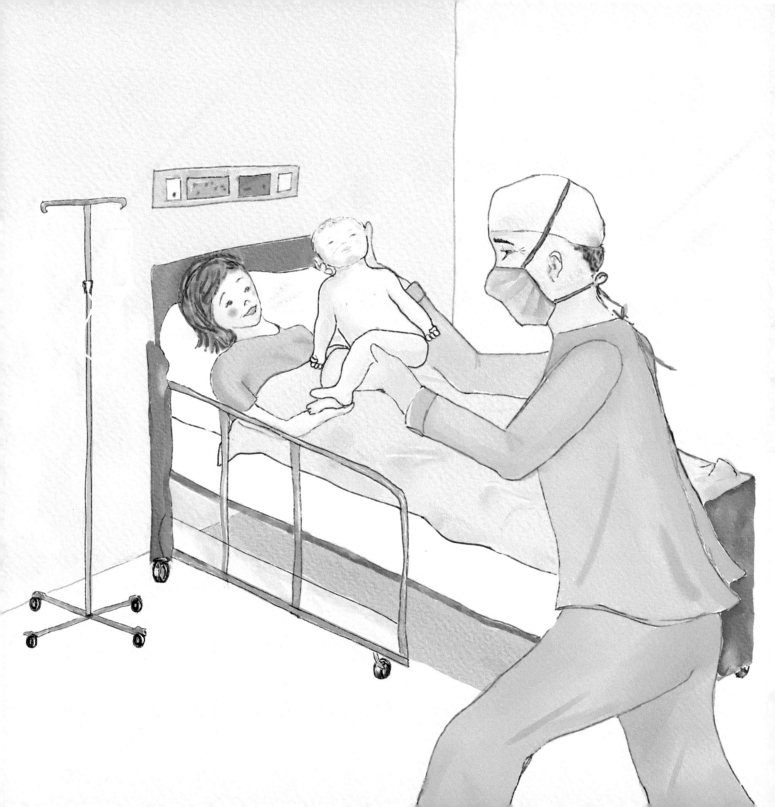

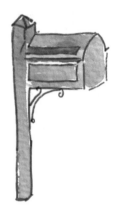

The announcement rings out,
"It's a boy!" or "A girl!"
And then from the moment
they enter the world,
boys will be boys and girls will be girls,
for that
is how
God planned it.

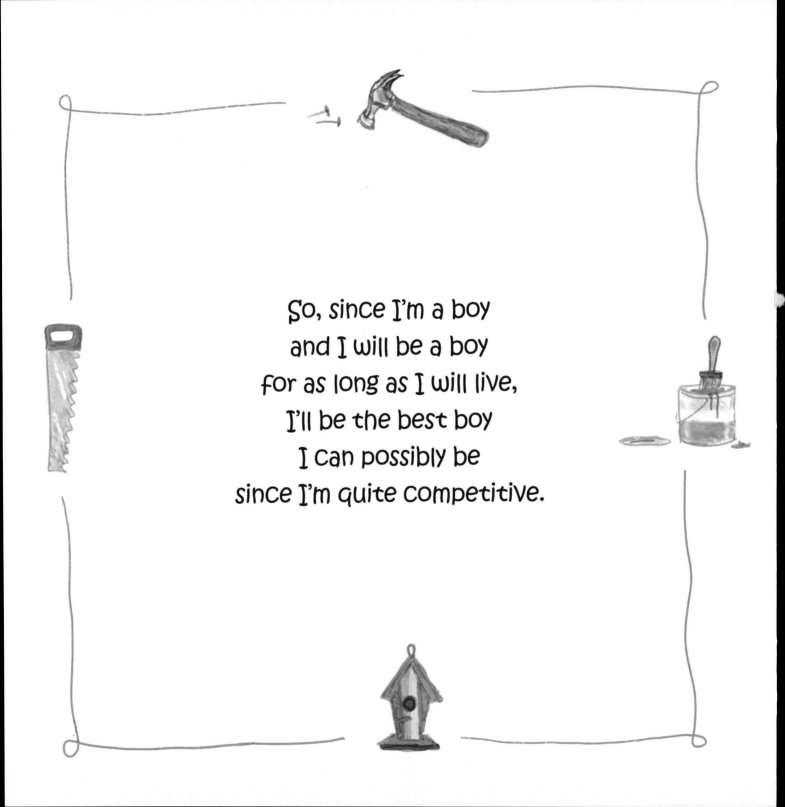

So, since I'm a boy
and I will be a boy
for as long as I will live,
I'll be the best boy
I can possibly be
since I'm quite competitive.

And when I grow up,
I will be a man.
I'll work hard, lead well,
and be caring.
I'll be a good husband,
and train my sons well
and be brave
though I might not be daring.

The announcement rings out,
"It's a boy!" or "A girl!"
And then from the moment
they enter the world,
boys will be boys and girls will be girls,
for that
is how
God planned it.

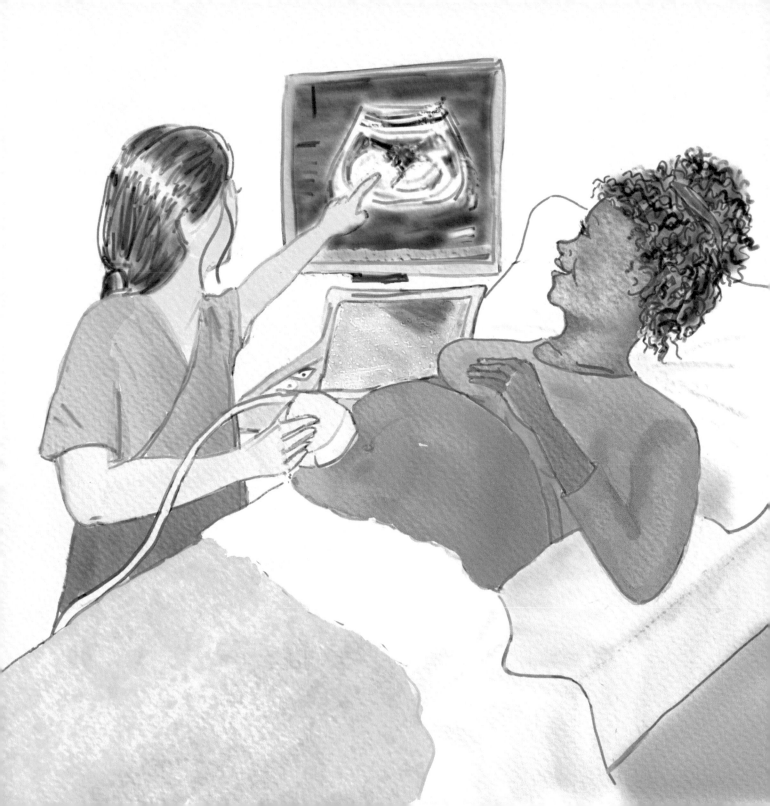

And when I'm all grown,
a woman I'll be
hardworking, supportive,
and good company.
My children I'll nurture,
I'll be a good wife.
I'll take care of my home
and serve God all my life.

So, since I'm a girl
and I will be a girl
for as long as I am alive,
to be the best girl
I can possibly be
is the goal
for which I will strive.

So, people have always
been boys or been girls
from the moment
they come into being.
And excitement has always
surrounded the news
once the image
or baby is seen.

You see, back at the start
when God made the first pair,
His own image He let them display.
And both man and woman
together did this,
and it's still that way today.

It's right at the core
of the person I am
in my body, my heart,
and my mind,
an important ingredient
God put in the mix
when I was uniquely designed.

I've been a girl
since God first thought me up,
even before I was born.
Since this is the plan
God intended for me,
it's not one that
I want to spurn.

Girls Will Be Girls

Ellie Owen

For my dearly loved Uncle Dennis

This book belongs to

_____

Printed in the United States
by Baker & Taylor Publisher Services